FAR AWAY FROM MY HEART

EVERGREEN DIARY

ISBN 979-888546153-5

EVERGREEN DIARY

Contents

Contents

Contents

Contents

Far away from my heart

The fun collaboration of this month's Evergreen Diary anthology brings you a journey of their hearts and a road to make this a successful project.

Acknowledgements

To all the selected writers, thankyou for being a part of this journey. To all who joined the anthology from the beginning and close to the deadline, your excitement and enthusiasm is much appreciated.

To the selection committee and the editorial team, your invaluable help made this anthology possible.

1. To the deleted selfie

To the deleted selfie,

It wasn't your fault, really. We tend to get rid of the things which didn't turn out as our expectations. In that one selfie , I was grinning, alot. I thought people would look at my teeth and call them imperfect.

There is nothing I can do except bury my love for you. People have raised the standards so high that my height won't reach it , no matter how hard I try to jump, higher each time.

Insecurities knocked and said "To say I LOVE YOU , one must know first how to say I" and made a leave. I is just an alphabet when it belongs to me, but when I've to talk as a first person, I don't know why something starting with I ends with you. It's never I love myself and always I love you.

Confidence is somewhere lost between midnight fears and tears. Amidst which confidence loses its energy and Insecurities are somehow louder, always. I now know why something like recycle bin exists, to give life to something which we tried to end, believing the standards raised by someone else are for us too. Except that they're not, we have our own standards for our own height.

You said I killed you , haunt me then.

Tumhe agar mujhme aur tujhme chunne ka mauka mile toh,
Tum khud ko hi chunna

- Priyanka Suthar

2. Him and hope

People come and go, the cycle keeps repeating. Can it stop for once , atleast when it was you who had to stay. Change is constant and that's the biggest irony of my life. When I go home carrying the world's weight on my head to find some peace it reminds me of you, says I'm not myself without you. It's taking revenge of my past, I'd tell my home that I don't feel at home without him and now home refuses to even recognise me without him.

Him and home were never different, I atleast believed I'd never find a need to seperate them. I loved coming home with him. Now I realise it was him who made my home actually home. My home betrays and asks for him in a way screaming "I'm not your home, your calling wrong house your home, it's him, it was always him". I have hopes of you returning, if not for me, atleast to make this house - home. My home misses you more than I miss home, you. Come back to home, will you?

While I was understanding home and him are the same, you tried your best to prove me wrong and I failed at it miserably. You remind me of me and my home that it's home and not just a four walled house.

Dear hope ,
Don't ever lose hopes on me, I'm trying my best.
POV - Him is a person called hope

- Priyanka Suthar

3. To the boy who reminds me of me

Pour rain over my rotten body, like you always did. You won't do it anymore, will you? You won't be here, I won't be here. Our words will remain, they'll get repeated everytime someone falls in love, to express thier love using the words we express our love.

Your name has more meaning about love than the word "love" will ever have.

It's tough to write about something you haven't experienced at all. A bit easier if you've imagined the scenarios in your heart a million times or maybe a little more or less. Love, for me is something like that.

I always mess up first things, the first Iloveyou was said to someone who didn't have a clue about my existence. What if I mess up love too? What if I mess up being in love with the person I love being myself the most? What if I mess up us? I don't think we are a happy tomorrow anymore, you and me.

I look at the box which is placed at a corner, or thrown away there. I search love in it, love in the torn photograph and the torn love letters. You can get rid of the love letters but you can't get rid of the love, can you? The love between the spaces of each word you wrote for me, about me? The love I can see in the photograph, your smile is still the same. Like I always told, reality with some fiction. Your smile feels so real and bright, it takes me to magical places, I didn't even know existed. Hence, reality with some fiction sprinkled.

Your memories have created a town in my heart which I can't help but visit each time I hear the word love, or any word. Everything reminds me of you. Can you stop it? Stop *a long pause* loving me. There, I said it.

From,
Someone, who is still a fan of your smile.

- Priyanka Suthar

4. Yeh khula aasmaan, aagaye hun kahan

I like to believe that clouds move a bit slower when I'm looking at them. In a way trying to say "We're here". But only for a while. And when they form beautiful shapes, trying to say "You're going to be okay"

I like the sun but sometimes it's too much to handle. The clouds cover it in a way to say "We got your back, mate"

I wonder if there is a way to say to them that it is okay to feel heavy sometimes. That it is okay to let it out if it gets a lot inside. That their tears are the second most beautiful ones I've ever seen. First, always remains his.

Dear clouds,
It's okay to just vanish sometimes. We understand. We can appreciate clear skies somedays. We miss you tho, just saying. This is just a small token of my heart that I'm giving you for being there for me. All the times I thought I'll die out of period cramps, miserable feeling of not being loved, not loving enough, not being there for people, them not being there for me and everything I've felt and all the things you

know already. Thanks for being there, beside or above me. And tolerating my emotional dramas.

From,
Someone, who has half of her gallery filled with your pictures.
XOXO

- Priyanka Suthar

5. On holding on to your younger self

Holding something delicate as her, my hand started to shiver. Almost as if to say "You have no rights to". Her lips moved, she whispered to make sure it was audible to me and only me. It was loud enough to me tho, loud enough to hurt me in my heart ; listening to that voice and what she had said, "Don't hold me, the last time you did you almost ended me". I'm not sure about that. I try saying to her that if I can start loving her she can too. She hardly seems convinced. I try to say better or atleast the right words and later add that life will one day happen and find her and that she'll fall in love with life as I did. More, everyday. I'm sure about that , afterall she's me and I'm her. I know her and I want her to know me too. That I survived everything she thinks she can't. I made it through the tunnel and saw the bright side of it. I want her to be happy for me like I'm for her. I want her to know that the things she's worrying about, no one cares once you're 19 or strong enough to accept them yourself. I want to say so much to her, all the things I'm proud of, happy for and love. Everything and anything. She can just sit there and wonder how I made it through with so much confidence. She can stare at me in awe when I tell her about my beautiful life and get irritated when I tell her about the dumb stuff I still do. She can just be here.

I wish I could say all this to her. I wish you knew me like I know you. I wish we knew who saved whom. Or it was us in a whole. I wish.

We save the love in a photograph. We try to keep everything alive in the photograph. Even the dead. Especially our younger selves.

- Priyanka Suthar

6. About the writer

About the writer:

Priyanka Suthar

Priyanka is someone who believes being kind and long walks are the only ways to get through life. She has been a reader for as long as she can remember. For her, words combine to form a different world. She belongs to that world. She loves sky, pretty houses, deep conversations and everything else she can call home. Sometimes people too. Emphasis on sometimes.

7. From us

From Bhavna Das (Editorial Team)
to Priyanka Suthar:

—

"Her X-factor comes in when you pause between the lines to understand what happened. The moment you go back to the stanza, the deepness in the words makes itself visible."

8. Spaces between us

Love is hidden among the places that we overlook,

standing by the corner, you look over the street,

Among the strangers that walk past in front of you,

The rain that falls unplanned,

hiding under the small umbrella, shirts getting soaked,

You stand under the tree,

branches swaying back and forth

as the wind gushes past them,

so heavy, but the breeze falls so light on your face,

At the corner of the street

you see a father catching his daughter in his arms,

And for a moment this act feels so poignant,

and you wonder if love like this actually exists.

You see a woman and a man,

barely able to hide under the bus stand,

with their hands engulfed in each other's and love is existing

between them.

There stands an old man, holding a bouquet of white lily's in

one and

a wet cake box in the other and his partner just a couple of

feet away

They laugh so intimately that the love between them grows

closer with every drop of rain
Maybe love is all about existing, about being patient,
And love is different for everyone,
And maybe it is just around the corner
or maybe it is far, far away,
And it is in the rain, the sun and the moon,
And it is in the meal you made for yourself
after a tiring day, or in the cup of tea you drink
while watching the rain wash away the world of its misery
And maybe it is in this letter I write to you,
not hoping it reaches you
And maybe, just maybe,
between our worlds.

- Saisha Bhargav

9. Sailors delight

In the early hours of the evening,
I let myself become all the colours of the sky.
These days the rain makes the clouds utterly grey,
and I wonder why my chest drowns itself with love,
pain, tenderness and anger.
I let myself become the sky, so why won't I?
I saw children playing in the park and as I walked past them,
between their shadows colliding with each other like the clouds.
Maybe it was a game I wasn't aware of.
I saw the childhood I knew.
I didn't feel sad for my childhood, I let myself become an admirer for a while.
Watching their hands push each other and their legs paddling the wheels,
until the adults drag them by their hands.
And I let myself go home with the same feet I used to run in the sand.
The sand washed away a long time ago,
but if I try, I can find the remains of my childhood
between these fingers that now write about them.

Somewhere along the way to my home,

I see my shadow colliding with the adult.
Dragging the child in me to home.
To bed. To eat food.
I carry myself to bed, and find myself shifting on one side of
the bed tonight.
Maybe the memories lay heavy,
their grip on the swing was too tight,
That my memories now lay there tighter than ever.
The bed gets warmer, and the memories soon leave the bed.
And tonight under the cloudy sky,
under the rain, they run out to play,
to become a child again, where no adult lives.
But by the morning they hide in the hands of some other
child.
And someday I'll see them again.

- Saisha Bhargav

10. The coming of winters

In autumn, I suffer. In winter, I bloom.
There's something infuriating about this contrast.
The pollen in the air fill my eyes
And nose and leave me with an empty sigh.
The mist of winters makes my heart feel at ease.

The town was floating in the air,
as if it was consumed by the ocean,
multiple lighthouses to guide
At an arm's distance.

August dropped by like a humble old man
thanking you with a glint of pity
For himself in his eyes.
September came along
like a child with his innocent smile,
Their laugh echoing like a distant jazz melody
and you relive the moments you wished
Lasted all four seasons.
The old month disorients and the nature of
Newness overwhelms me now even more.

- Saisha Bhargav

11. For her

It's 1:55 AM and my brain is remembering all the missed out details of my conversations with her. Oh, she was pretty. A goddess, perhaps. She sounded like one. Not just her voice, but the way she thought of the world. Once, she asked her parents for a pair of chopsticks, and they handed her a fork. Isn't it better to eat with a fork rather than handling two sticks? That evening, she was furious. She told me how you can't replace the authenticity and the beauty of something just to make it simple. I agreed. One day, she told me she will be an artist, but she never drew after she left high school. The hands she drew were not proportional, and the head was just… a disaster. No, I did not tell her that. It was art.

Later that week, she told me she will write like Proust and talk about her memories and love and life. I wonder if she wrote about me. I told her I loved her one evening and she replied, You're my epiphany to a love that I never felt. Not only that, but I could try to trace you in this sky right now, but you'll outshine." Yes, she was trying to write poetry that week. I wonder what she meant. That evening we sat under the moon, and she sparkled like a star drunk with a potion made out of love, life, dead flowers and lavender. She was the brightest constellation, and I was an admirer, far away from the earth and afraid. She was the cello in that one song which, without words, was the star of the piece. The catch was, if you could hear her. Not too mainstream. She never liked anything mainstream except, stars. She tattooed stars on her back and asked me to trace a constellation once. I traced her name. How boring of you, she laughed. Only if she knew how beautiful her name looked as a constellation. She lives in my mind as the bright constellation that I admire once every cold night when the sky is hazy, and I wonder if she does it too.

- Saisha Bhargav

12. About the writer

<u>About the writer:</u>

Saisha Bhargav

Saisha is a philosophy student by day and a writer by the evening. When she is not spending time reading or writing she can be seen living the main character life vicariously through movies. She loves to write about the evanescent moments of the everyday life through the two characters living rent free in her mind.

13. From us

• 23 •

**From Sonali Sureka (Selection Committee)
to Saisha Bhargav :**

—

"She can go on using metaphors through her poems like expressing her joys and sorrows. It's the fusion of her words and expressive capabilities that makes her a good writer."

14. In my head

I've never met you
But I can't stop dream of you.
Your voice in my ears.
Your hands on my body.
Your lips on mine.
All I do is dreaming of the day it will be possible
And I hope you do too
Because now that you're in my head
All I want is to be in your head too.

- Marie Mokrani

15. Here

I've never met you
But I can't stop dream of you.
Your voice in my ears.
Your hands on my body.
Your lips on mine.
All I do is dreaming of the day it will be possible
And I hope you do too
Because now that you're in my head
All I want is to be in your head too.

- Marie Mokrani

16. So far

So far yet so closed

How can we live in 2 different continent

But Love each other so deeply.

Nowadays, we become closer

To the ones who live

At the other side of the world,

While distancing ourselves

From the ones who lives with us.

That is the blessing as the curse of internet.

- Marie Mokrani

17. About the writer

About the writer:

Marie Mokrani

Marie is a french woman of 23 years old. She is passionate about mental health, nutrition and all form of self-care. She started writing poetry to express all what she was keeping for herself; the good, the bad and her dreams, hoping her writings would inspire and heal people like it does with he

18. From us

• 31 •

From Kashish Garg (Selection Commitee) to
<u>Marie Mokrani:</u>

—

"She knows what she is writing and going for. She isn't bothered by the number of words. She can go long or by a short write-up if given a choice, and that will barely change the outcome."

19. A burning theatre

As she danced
To the silent screams of her agony
Eyes dazed
Lips tinted in a venomous glaze
A fortune caked her face
As tears rolled down
Her excellent face
The show must go on

- Ona

20. Furnace

The cup's about to break
It's been there for years
Slapped shaped moulded
Heated brazed tested
It survived
Carries a part of itself
The cup's about to break
Endeared, reminiscent
It holds still
For the water to splash around
Unsteady,
A pacifier
The cup's about to break
It's shaking from the force
The responsibility
The cup's about to break

- Ona

21. Hello? Are you there?

Friendships fade

Smiles grow rarer

Leg bounces up and down

We're growing up

Assignments get harder

All my nails are chewed out

No one laughs in class anymore

We're growing up

Skin of my thumb is scratched raw

Dark circles get darker

Nothing out of the ordinary

We're growing up

Darkness seems familiar

Winters get lonely

Shine a light through the dark

We're growing up

Nostalgia hits once a while

Scented candle fills my lungs

Subtle silence in my ears

Fingers hitting keys echoes in the room

It's okay

We're growing up

- Ona

22. About the writer

About the writer:

Ona Dubay

Ona is always explicitly explaining random psychological theories or quoting dramatic gay drama/play dialogues, if not working on her mental health mission. Her poetry is an attempt to put raw emotions into words - a task indeed. She hopes that the expression of emotions (as poetry) can help destigmatize mental health, and help people give their mental health the attention it deserves.

23. From us

From Bhavna Das (Editorial Team) to
<u>**Ona Dubay**</u> **:**

—

"She is a wonderful storyteller. Her words capture a particular essence that is scattered around the whole story, ultimately making the writers very curious to read further."

24. Tell Me All The Ways To Love You

I may never know how to love someone without giving my heart as the first thing you'll strew. And I know that you'll give love a different flare too. You'll say that love always makes people weak. That it takes away parts of me and laughs back at what I've given. But love itself would leave one day and I'll swallow back the urge to say:

"I hope you realize where we all went wrong. I hope you realize that I'll be gone by the time you need me and there's no way back to me again. I hope you learn to hold someone's heart in the palm of your hands and not let it fall apart."

So that when I wake up choking on back sobs, searching for a stranger in my bed, I'll tell myelf how love could come to me in different forms. Yet I'll choose to stay. I'll stay till these red flags feel more like home. I'll stay till you look me in the eye and say that you see nothing but forgiveness. Because if there's anything that I want than necessary, I want to love someone nothing like I loved you. I want to lay my heart like it's the first thing only you could devour.

- Sandali Pathirana

25. I Wonder If I'd Be Happy Again

Some may say that it's narcissism,

But I teach myself how to kiss myself in the mirror,

Because for someone who has nothing to lose,

I want to give myself the love I gave you--

So I tell myself that loving from a distance is still love,

Because I was lonelier loving you than when I needed to love myself,

But I still think back to how you made me feel,

How it still makes this abandoned of a body shudder at the slightest inconvenience,

Realizing I was in love with only an idealized version of you,

How you misspelled love like it really wasn't me but your best friend--

The next day you get me think that it was just a spur-of-the-moment kind of love,

You tell me that we're very much alike,

When you never really hesitated to let me go.

But I still like to think of what we could've been instead,

I still like to think that we accepted each other for who we truly were,

But on the face of it,

You really couldn't settle for less.

Less of a daughter who had her heart broken into scriptures
of a film.
Or perhaps your lover whose name flowed merely and in vain,
Just in vain~

- Sandali Pathirana

26. Teach Me How To Go To Hell

In a world where people fight for someone to love them, they don't love themselves anymore. They hold love in the palm of their hands and let it go like fireflies wanting to make the sky colorfully warm again. And then they complain. They complain about loving each other like it's the only thing to have done right. Till love would keep them wounded and they would be just fine. Till you remind yourself what hate feels like. How it still feels a lot like love.

- Sandali Pathirana

27. Too Sad To Cry

I'm certain about being less worthy of everything that your
eyes yearn to see--
My body once seemed to me,
a dreamscape,
a fortress that cloisters little girls like me,
more immaculate than my mind would ever accept.
It is now more a movie that tucked away my words,
an abandoned homeland than possibly any other country or
continent,
and nothing is as loathsome and unviable as a home that is
strewn to its blueprints.
But today,
I woke up wanting to kiss you,
thinking back to when her name curled on your tongue like it
has never been the same about me.
Which is to say:
I'll never kiss the ground just the same,
I'll never own it like I ever did,
I'll never call it the lover I always needed,
Yet I'll love it further away from these clouds,
And even if this room makes me feel like I can't breathe
anymore,
I'll choose to say nothing like it,

I'll choose to live instead--

- Sandali Pathirana

28. About the writer

About the writer:

Sandali Pathirana

When the world gives no answers, Sandali confides in her words than escape. Best described, writing is both her home and battlefield. She is unapologetically devoted to her love for poetry, often found questioning every facet of life, fuelled by honesty and compassion to find a higher sense of purpose -- that is inner fulfillment. Quite frankly, writing is her love language.

29. From us

From Kashish Garg (Selection Commitee)
to <u>Sandali Pathirana</u> :

—

"Her poetries are pretty straight yet have some hidden meanings. She follows her heart and walks where it leads her to. And to a writer, that is nothing less than a gift."

30. My night falls

As the night falls
Darkly and deeply
The sky goes black,

The memory
Of yours,
In my mind
Goes brighter
Slowly and sharply,

Your thoughts
Grab my soul,
Took it to
Another world
My world,
Where I can be I
And you can be you
The way we are,
The way we love,
Without the fear of
Losing one other,
Without the fear of the
Outer world,

I can hold your hand there
And kiss your forehead,
And hug you
Without regretting if any body is watching me.

- Vaibhavi Bhadouriya

31. Suno

Jara Suno yun door to jaa rahe ho
Par wapas aane par hum na mile
To udaas mat hona....

Tum jab chaho bol dete ho kuchh bhi,
Hum se puchho kya gujarti hogi hum par...

Tumse pyar karne me itane aage nikal aaye he
Ab na tum ho or na koi or he
Bas hum he tanhaa ekdum akele....

Toote hue ko bikherna ho to,
Ghaw nahi bus chot hi kafi he....

Ishq to sab karte he,
Maslaa to ye he jatata kon he or nibhaata kon.

- Vaibhavi Bhadouriya

32. About the writer

<u>About the writer:</u>

Vaibhavi Bhadouriya

Vaibhavi is an introvert but extrovert with her people, a science student with inclination towards arts. Loves to spend her spare time playing with words, drawing random thoughts on paper, listening to her favourite playlist and enjoying quality time with her people.

33. From us

From Bhavna Das (Editorial Team) to
<u>Vaibhavi Bhadouriya:</u>

—

"She masks her words with metaphors, describing life itself as a small part of the cosmos."

34. as they're the Guardians

Everyone said,
We've come a long way since
the Old Days,
memorizing yore
adorable remembrances
little hands over them,
covered us as
the tree doesn't allow the rays to come in,
showering love
giving endorsements, And
loving us always selflessly
and after all their sacrifices,
we've become nothing but
selfish.

when you were a child
they were the guardian,
you've become an adult
they are still your guardian,
now you've become selfish
but they are still the ones
who loves you selflessly,

As they are the Guardians.

not valued, not cherishing them
what they've done to us,
we left everything all
up to them,
That's rubbish.
Somedays, they're hard up,
not by the cash,
but by the emotions, by the faith
and by the belief.
but again, as usual,
they put on the same smile,
start loving us selflessly,
As they're the Guardian!

- Arshi Gautam

35. i love you desperately!

i love you Desperately,
painting or writing or
whatever I do,
i imagine you in the work
and get a better light.

your frequency matches my vibe,
Kind of,
Ahh no! I'm sure here.
You're away from me "NOW"
but there's a HOPE, "SOON"
hope, i have the hope
hope, i have the patience

i love you Desperately,
waiting for your message,
giving water to plants
feels like to breathe
because there is hope.
As a plant will become a tree,
so does I'll become more of you,
waiting for you, with all my patience, with all my HEART!

i love you desperately,
with patience and love,
take the moon for you,
practicing "I LOVE YOU"

Oh God, it's always you,
now please,
change this "SOON" to "NOW"
waiting!

- Arshi Gautam

36. Kal ho na ho

Kya pata kal ho na ho,

Do pal zara aur muskuralo,

Kabhi beparwah hoke,

To kabhi betanhan hoke,

Jhadte balo ki fikar na karke,

In balo ko, maddham si chalti

Is hawa main, tum mila lo,

Apni ye chalti saanse zara

mehsoos to karke dekho,

Mano dobara ek zindagi ka ehsaah hoga,

Ye zindagi, asal main kuch hi pal ki aur hai,

Khul ke jeelo thora aur

Kya pata kal ho na ho!

- Arshi Gautam

37. Apology

That path was rough,
on which I stepped.
The Journey was Tough!

I'm putting down about this now still,
feeling nervous.
I forgot who I'm!
and that's all happened after walking on that road that should
haven't taken but actually, that was taken!

I'm not able to explain it,
but the only solution here is to
apologize to me!
Because of the way I walked, I've brought judgmental eyes for
me, for my body, for my mind, for my soul, for my creativity,
for my talent, for my happiness, and my soul!
I became like, " a happy face everywhere, but the heart full
of disappointments" because that was the moment where I
became like the world, allowed others to disrespect me, to
spoil my peace, and sometimes they did let me down!
But from now onwards, I realized that I'm okay with being
me! My body is perfect, my scars are beautiful, I love it when
I smile and I appreciate those efforts which I've imposed on

me, to be a better person!
That was a very difficult phase,
although it taught me a lot and at last,
I'm proud of who I'm.
I'm the happiest ever! :-)
-that only matters

- Arshi Gautam

38. About the writer

About the writer:

Arshi Gautam

Shruti (her real name is Arshi) is an artist who doesn't crave perfection. She believes that art is all about Creation. 24/7 dreamer. She loves smiling. Her spare time is spent writing poems and for her, poems have been her second home. She loves dancing, listening to music, long walks, deep conversation, and spending nights under the shade of the Moon.

39. From us

From Riya Kaur (Editorial Team) to
<u>**Arshi Gautam :**</u>

—

"She's definitely a feeler in her stories searching for a home. Her write-ups makes me nostalgic about something I never even had, like a feeling I follow to reach somewhere that only exists between her stories."

40. You need you

Over the years I have realised one thing very strongly,
that no one can heal you for surely.

If you want yourself to be mended,
then be ready to be alone and fended.

They will come listen and advice,
but not all of them have their intensions wise.

They will feel sad and obviously pretend,
because they don't want your beginning but only end.

It is you who wants to and will have to rise,
and for this be ready to pay the price.

Nothing in this world comes for free,
you have to buy and bow the seed in order to grow the tree.

Don't feel bad and allow the time to resurrect you.
hard times are part of life and you will get through.

I have seen people pulling it off from the ashes,
just like cricket converting chances into catches.

- Aditi Dewra

41. Ek jahaan aisa banana hai

Ek jahaan aisa banana hai,
Dharti par swarg sajana hai,
Daulat ki jahan zaruraat nahi,
Bas pyaar kamana hai ,
Ek jahaan aisa banana hai...

Jahan oouch neech ki soch na ho,
Burai ki jahan pahunch na ho,
Dil se rishto ko nibhana hai,
Ek jahaan aisa banana hai...

Jahan dil mein acchai palti ho,
Dusro ki tarakki na khalti ho,
Khudgarzi ko bhulana hai,
Ek jahaan aisa banana hai...

Jahan sab saath mil ke rehte ho,
Izzat se baat kehte ho,
Shikwe bhula ke sabko apnana hai ,

Ek jahaan aisa banana hai...

Jahan nafrat ki aandhi nahi,
Bas pyaar ki hawa chalti ho,
Jahan siskiya nahi sirf hassi hi goonjti ho,
Poori duniya ko apne saath hasana hai,
Ek jahaan aisa banana hai...

Jahan Surat nahi sirat ko log saware ,
Chehre ko nahi mann ko nikhare,
Chehre ko nahi Mann ko chamkana hai,
Ek jahaan aisa banana hai...

Jahan na kisi ki haar aur na kisi ki jeet ho,
Sab saath ho aur dosti ke geet ho,
Aisa rang jamana hai,
Ek jahaan aisa banana hai...

Jahan na koi jati na dharam ho,
Sabka khuda unka karam ho,
"Tera mera mera tera" inse khud ko bachana hai,
Ek jahaan aisa banana hai...

Jahan dilo mein doori na ho,
Koi khwaish adhoori na ho,
Jahan humne ek dooje ka Sahara ban Jana hai,
Ek jahaan aisa banana hai.

- Aditi Dewra

42. Kasoor

Aasmaan me chamkne vale sitare hi toh hote hai...
Lehre ko jinki talash h vo kinare hi to hote h..
Agar khwaish karte chaand ki to vo bhi mil jata,
Pr amawas ki raat me,
vo bhi khi kho jata..
Waqt ke sath badalte rehna hi toh jindagi ka dastoor hai...
Fir jo badal jate h log waqt ke saath,
Unka kya kasoor h.

- Aditi Dewra

43. About the writer

About the writer:

Aditi Dewra

Aditi is a limitless and innocent person for meaning. She is a person who always likes spending nights alone under the shade of a full moon and an open sky full of glittery stars. She believes in the power of love. Obsessed with Music. She loves chasing sunrise and sunsets, living on an unhealthy dose of movies and cold coffee.

44. From us

From Sonali Sureka (Selection Committee) to Aditi Dewra:

—

"Her poems are about the other side of things - the struggles, the heartbreaks and how one survives through life, all the journey described in a raw interpretation played in of her mind."

45. At night

What keeps you up at night?
I was up late thinking about his sight
In the middle of the night
Honey brown eyes
A wonderfully sad smile.

—

What makes you not sleep at night?
The ordeal of sleeping still
An incubus under the bed
Hiding in the darkness of the night
And as soon as I switch off the light
It becomes alive.

—

Why are you not sleeping yet?
Not seeing the nightmare you should have seen and be fret
Avoiding the nightmares
I stay upright at night
Playing songs on repeat in my mind
Acting like it won't cause any strife
Taking long strides
And staying up at midnight.
- Apurva Kumari

46. Break Apart

Hold me close, share same air
You still feel far away
Can't make things clear.
It's blurry outside
The tears cloud my eyes
Cheeks felt damp
And mind felt numb
Can't hear your voice
It's too damn far
Hold me close, don't break my heart.

—

Can't say a word
But I feel it all
My mind's so full
With an aching heart.
I'll hold you close
Will make you laugh
I won't let go
With a breaking heart.

—

The blizzard in snow
Won't keep us apart
Stay this way

Don't break my heart.
It effing hurts
We can't fall apart
Hold me close, it's too damn dark
Can't see the light
So guide me past
I can't see anything
It's too damn dark

—

Take my breath
Tear me apart
Can't see you there
In the dark
I'm soo numb
And it's dark
Can't find you
We fell apart

—

You say you love
You say you care
But I don't feel love
And you don't care.
- Apurva Kumari

47. Portrait of a lady

I'm an imagination. A mind and soul trapped in a body of illusion. I'm a creation, someone's mind's deterrence. Most illusionistic likeness of a mother, sister, daughter, aunt, wife and grandma. But these things don't define me cause at the end I'm mere a being, a human being like yourself trapped in this body, an image painted by the society. But my soul is genderless and it knows nothing less than just love. Not the love of a mother, sister, daughter, or wife but the love beyond all. Self love. You try to shame me cause of my gender, paint me red because you believe I've no color. But how ironic that this body made of nothing but blood and flesh is noting but me as I'm red. You say you want no part of me that I'm filth an abomination in the society because I'm not capable of protecting myself, containing myself. You say this but I need to protect myself from no one but you. I can't contain myself because you won't let me because you also know you don't want me to have a mind or a soul but just as a furniture in your home. But you who is made of someone like me, a woman, when separated from me there remains noting of you. I'm your mother, sister, wife & daughter but I'm also beyond your imagination. I'm a portrait of a lady.
- Apurva Kumari

48. About the writer

About the writer :

Apurva Kumari

The name Apurva means 'something which did not exist before or is newly born' and she tries to abide by it spreading the commonly different ideas and thoughts and still believing in the impossibilities that the future beholds for us all. She believes in art, literature, words, moon, romance and every earthly thing ever created by the nature.

49. From us

**From Riya Kaur (Editorial Team)
to <u>Apurva Kumari</u> :**

—

"Her writings have that magic you find when you visit your favorite place after ages. Its nostalgic, relatable, filled with emotions that surfaces after every line. She keeps her write-ups short while expressing what she needs to, and that is a rare trait."

50. The Life Sailor

Just like a sailor sails
Even in the most turbulent weather
Even after losing some co-sailors
Even after leaving behind those lovely villagers

—

The Villagers
Who enrich the sailor with experience
Who aid the sailor during turbulence
Who provide the sailor with shelter
Who nourish the sailor with fodder.

—

Just like the sailor sails
The journey of life prevails
The tides take us away
Adding memories along the way

—

The Memories
With an ocean of people we meet
With a sea of personalities we greet
With a river of lives we touch
With a pond of friends we clutch

—

The Friends
We learn from and we teach
We gain from and we give
We build with and we break
We forgive and sometimes we even forget

—

Then again some day
Those memories shine
Like the treasure the sailor finds
Meanwhile
The next village seems to be in sight
The next set of adventures shine bright
The sailor adjusts the sail
Ready to write yet another tale.
- Swetapadma Narayani Acharya

51. A Smile I Am

smile I am
That lights up your face
After the darkest of days
Through the tears in your eyes
I emerge as a victor fighting all lies

—

A smile I am
Who fights all hurdles
Fills you with strength through your troubles
To convey that you will win
You have the courage within

—

A Smile I am
Which can transmit in a second
From one kind face to other
Whether they are unknown or a friend.

—

A smile I am
That brings twinkle to your eyes
When the dress you wanted fits your size
That brings joy to your soul
When you smell your favorite food and you can't control

—

A smile I am
Who brings peace to your heart
When you see me start
Curving the lips on their face
'Coz you were better than the people they met

—

A smile I am
Which makes you thrilled
When your parents have me
Marking your success in your field

—

A smile I am
That everyone deserves
That gives you pleasures
That is full of treasures

—

And I promise you to stay
To fight your battles along the way
Till the time you cherish me
In these tiny little moments everyday !
- Swetapadma Narayani Achary

52. About the writer

<u>About the writer</u> :

Swetapadma Narayani Acharya

An enthusiastic girl hailing from the temple city, Bhubaneswar, with a keen interest of diving deep into human thinking, thus pursuing Psychology Hons. With a love for food, songs and literature, she seeks her daily dose of motivation from spreading smiles around her. She believes that our actions and accomplishments speak in volumes about ourselves and thus strives to do her best.

53. From us

From Sonali Sureka (Selection Committee) to
<u>Swetapadma Narayani Acharya :</u>

—

"Her poetry takes me back to the younger times when I was newly fond of it. She doesn't go for much complex metaphors or ironies, rather she keeps it to the point and crafts it pretty steadily, becuase to her, a good poem is about expressing with the right words, not the long ones."

54. The world is a Masquerade

Each day you wear a mask,

hiding yourself from others.

Too insecure from the truth to embark

the journey that wrecks the zones of comfort, that bothers

you and all the sheep around.

So you wear a mask and

hide the truth underground.

Making the world a unique Masquerade,

With you and sheep dancing

a meek rigid dance, round and round and round.

And you call the different a sinful soul

hiding under the mask you call, the amour of God.

You envy deep inside to those who are naked

with no truth and lies.

As you know you are dead inside the

mask that suffocated the lives

of millions who chose the easy path, wearing a pall

making a world a unique masquerade ball

with that meek rigid dance.

So go round and round and round.

- Raunak Singh

55. Life

Life, what is it?
A journey so musical
Or the Pandora's gift.
Many come and go
finding its meaning for ages
Many tried to explain it like the seven stages.
But do we really live?
Is the question so far
Is life is just a so called suffering
Or bliss at the altar
With we in the puppets play Playing our roles
dancing around the center
Being the center all along
So play by your own rules
make the choices you want
it may be not be simple
But it will be worthwhile and your own.
- Raunak Singh

56. About the writer

About the writer :

Raunak Singh

Raunak is an introverted person who likes spending nights alone under the shade of full moon and an open sky full of glitery stars. He loves painting, writing poems, reading and writing fiction about supernatural and life, death and society. He loves freedom of individual and appreciates divesrsity among people.

57. From us

From Bhavna Das (Editorial Team) to
<u>**Raunak Singh**</u> **:**

—

"He masks his words with metaphors, describing life itself as a small part of the cosmos."

58. Dear younger self

Dear younger self,

I miss you. I miss your presence.

Yes, I miss being myself. I miss those days when I was used to be cheerful and happy,I knew what i wanted, I used to listen to my heart and most importantly i had a solution to all of my problems.I miss those days when eating and sleeping were the only two activities i did. I had a clear and transparent mind then.Almost every little thing around me provided me a tint of happiness.

Well,its not the same anymore.Things have changed with time.Now,my mind has been cluttered with endless amount of stuff.I don't know what i want from life. I am clueless about everything.Now,everything is so puzzled and blurred.

Sometimes, I wish i never grew old. Adulting is making me feel lost and insane. I don't feel myself anymore.Everyday, when I wake up there is something going on inside my mind.I don't remember the last time i smiled happily. My life has become dull and monotonous. Sometimes, I think i should get a break from everything and chill but that never works.Everything is so unpredictable.Sometimes i just wish to disappear and i feel no one would be bothered by my absence. I love collecting souvenirs. I don't collect them anymore. I just sit with my collection and go back to the flashbacks. I remember how chirpy I used to be earlier. I used to attend all social get-togethers and parties and meet everyone with a jovial face. Nowadays, I just look for reasons to avoid any kind of social interaction. Earlier, I used to be optimistic about everything but now my mind doesn't let me think anything positive.

But you know what? Maybe all this is just a phase. Maybe, i'll get over it soon and feel myself again. Maybe I'll get to know what i actually want to do in my life.

Maybe I'll find the solutions to my problems again. Maybe I'll start collecting souvenirs again. Maybe I'll start meeting people again. Maybe I'll be happy again.

Maybe everything will get better with time.

Maybe?

—

- Saswati Vaniprava

59. Wo pehli baarish

Garmi ka mausam tha.Charo taraf bas loo chal rahi thi aur log pasine se lathpath ho chuke the.Pashu-Pakshi paani ki ek boond ke liye taras rahe the.Ped-Podhe paani ki raah dekhte-dekhte murjha gaye the.Main aur mere parivar ke sadasya balcony mein baithkar mausam ka halchal radio pe sun rahe the. Achanak se mere chehre par ek boond paani gira.Maine upar dekha kahin chhat se paani toh nahi tapak raha.Phir jo ek ke baad ek paani ke boondo ki barsaat hui mere dil ko jaise maano thandak hi pohanch gayi. Gagan me badal nritya karne lage.Sara parivar khushi se jhoomne laga.Ped-Podhon ko jaise jaan hi mil gayi. Mitti ki wo anokhi khushbu soongkar mann ko tripti mil gayi.Tabhi dadi adrak wali chai aur pakode lekar aai.Humne chai ki chuski lekar pehli baarish ki khushi achhe se manaai.Kuch der baad baarish ruk gayi.Pashu-Pakshi apni pyaas bujhane lage. Aasmaan ki taraf dekha toh ek aakarshak indradhanush nazar aaya. Wo khoobsurat drishya aaj tak meri aakhon mein sangrahit hai.
- Saswati Vaniprava

60. The girl at the shore

She smiles like the sea full of spirit
Her presence is like God's gift
Her hair colour is blond
Wandering here and there like a vagabond
Every now and then she's in my mind
Oh lord why did you make her so kind
She smells like fresh chamomile
Her heart's so pure and full of life
Spreading smiles everywhere
She walks towards the shore with no fear
Fire in her soul, tipsy are her eyes
Am so in awe of her, still in surprise
Sunrays falling on her face
She symbolises serendipity and grace
Suddenly she comes towards me
I am not able to hide my glee
"Will you click a picture of me?", she said
Spellbound by her I nodded my head
As she poses, my adrenaline rushes
An alluring scenery my eye catches
The camera fails to capture such beauty
I feel blessed to witness this deity
The way she runs her fingers through her hair

I can't stop looking at her and admire.
She walks through the waves like an angel
While I wonder "Oh lord, is she for real?"
- Saswati Vaniprava

61. About the writer

About the writer :

Saswati Vaniprava

Saswati loves long beach walks and evening hues. She's an avid reader and often gets lost expressing in her writeups. With a passion to experience the beauty that lies outside her comfort zone she's always ready for it with the right song.

62. From us

From Riya Kaur (Editorial Team) to
<u>Saswati Vaniprava</u> :

—

"She's definitely a feeler in her stories searching for a home. Her write-ups makes me nostalgic about something I never even had, like a feeling I follow to reach somewhere that only exists between her stories."

63. My eulogy to myself :

My eulogy to myself :
she passed away eating her last fries,
at the age of 203,
Left her belongings to her dogs,
That's the way she wanted to leave.
she was reckless, unbreakable, and fierce
like her poems,
the poem where people leave her,
much more than they loved her.
she was a careless fool,
fell in love with him,
knowing it'd set her on fire.
she wanted to itch poetry,
on snow-capped Mountains,
with words that turn,
a shy shade of pink,
the color of her palm
when she pinches tightly.
she was the shattered piece,
of the glittering moon,
hanging in the night sky,
reflected in the midnight ocean,
in liquid gold.

poetry was her hiding place,
where she was paper-thin,
her fears are the,
howls of many wolves.
how pain made her open the temple of her
heart,
and allow hatred to walk in,
wearing wet, muddy shoes.
she was made up of apologies
and unsent letters most quiet,
hiding in the quietest corners of the room,
overflowing and gleaming out of every slit.
(I want this to be read when I'm on my death bed)
- Sanjana Seth

64. The one that got away

your absence is becoming a habit for me now.
your absence
tastes like old coins swaying inside my mouth
but I started finding peace in it.
thought it was just a phase,
but now you became my lyricist.

—

your presence was home
but now I fear difference
I can weep alone, but I think
I will go numb in your presence,
I told you lights makes me happy,
but darkness is now my comfort zone.
since you're gone,
I let my mind take me,
someplace new as long as,
it's a place I haven't been with you.
your love was the worst hangover,
I ever had
pretending to be sober
realizing still not so over,
to dance in the doomed brace.

—

I write poetry,

on broken people.

wondering if you are broken,

or is it me who's broken?

remember,

you always loved it

when I wrote to you

keep writing,

you said

now I wonder if I'll ever be able to stop writing about you.

maybe not,

because this is my way to show

that I'm heartbroken,

you bring out all the poems in me.

—

I wouldn't say that I was surprised, no

I saw it coming

I saw that you had her clenched inside of your fist.

being with you was locking myself away in a room.

And haunting my shadows convincing myself that it was you.

I'm afraid if she dips the straw,

drinks all our memories from your eyes.

don't make her eat the poems

that I wrote for you. (the one you loved)

- Sanjana Seth

65. Loving you is like

Loving you is like -
chewing gum staying for 5 years in my digestive system,
sticking to my heart and getting caught in my ribcage,
for more time than you deserve.
increasing my anxiety day by day and
With that my grumpiness,
Reaching a point where I feel it heavy in my heart and fraud
in my smiles.
The falls season,
the leaves fell and so did I
Fell apart thinking about you.
Drowning,
I never learned how to swim,
All I learned was to use my hands and feet,
And When I met you my hands and legs were tied. Blooming,
when you smiled at me
But now becoming one of the thousands of thorns of cactus.
Living in dungeons toxicity,
It's sad coming out of it never ends.
Making my soul soggy,
Like a wet napkin after a cup of coffee has fallen in love with
the floor.

some days I'm not so fond of myself because the night you broke my heart I ended up turning my anger into poetry.
- Sanjana Seth

66. About the writer

About the writer:

Sanjana Seth

Sanjana is a law student halfway to her 20s and she's over it. her spare time is spent writing poems and listening to angry music. she loves chasing sunsets and sniffing books, living on an unhealthy dose of movies and cold coffee. she can turn anger into poetry.

67. From us

**From Riya Kaur (Editorial Team) to
Sanjana Seth :**

—

"She always has the perfect words to describe what she wants to convey. She questions the obvious in some other way and her melody lies in making everything poetic."